A Guide for Developing Your
Evangelistic Small Group

The Small Group Evangelism Planner

A Guide for Developing Your
Evangelistic Small Group

The Small Group Evangelism Planner

DR. JOHN R. SCONIERS, II

Printed in the United States of America

ISBN-13: 979-8-9862047-2-7

Real Moments Media
1385 Wilmington Way Suite 100
Grayson, GA 30017
www.realmomentsmedia.com

Dedicated in memory of my father, John R. Sconiers, Sr., my wife, Nicole, my mom, Maybell, and my children. Thank You for your continued support and prayers in everything that is accomplished!

The fruit of the righteous is a tree of life, And one who is wise gains souls.

Proverbs 11:30

Contents

Preface

Though your beginning was insignificant,
Yet your end will increase greatly.

Job 8:7 NASB

"Everything has a beginning"

C hristian denominations generally have low growth rates and stagnant evangelistic programs. While churches struggle to evangelize new believers, evangelistic models that utilize small group methodology have shown various degrees of success. However, regardless of the methodology, utilizing small groups generally almost always leads to success. *The Small Group Evangelism Planner* seeks to provide a framework for creating small groups so the reader can develop and execute their own personal evangelistic small group. This workbook was created to either stand along or accompany the authors original book, *The Small Book on Small Group Evangelism*. The author's intention was to create a document that could aid the user in the successful creation of an evangelistic small group. My prayer is that it aids the reader in fulfilling the role God has for you in the great commission.

Introduction

The grass withers, the flower fades, But
the word of our God stands Forever!

Isaiah 40:8 NASB

"Challenged, but God is still with us!"

After his resurrection, Jesus Christ gave the
Great Commission in Matthew 28:16-20:

16 But the eleven disciples proceeded to Galilee, to the mountain which Jesus had designated. 17 When they saw Him, they worshiped Him; but some were doubtful. 18 And Jesus came up and spoke to them, saying, "All authority has been given to Me in heaven and on earth. 19 Go therefore and make disciples of all the nations, baptizing them in the name of the Father and the Son and the Holy Spirit, 20 teaching them to observe all that I commanded you; and lo, I am with you always, even to the end of the age. NASB

Jesus instructed His eleven remaining disciples and followers to evangelize and grow the church. However, to embark on this endeavor, Jesus promised the disciples they would receive supernatural assistance (John 14, Acts 2). On the day of Pentecost, the Holy Spirit descended upon the disciples. Peter, one of Jesus's eleven disciples, began to witness with boldness to the multitude who gathered. Peter hoped that the individuals' hearts would be pricked as their conscience brought on a feeling of guilt and remorse. When the multitude asked what they should do in response to Peter's witness, Peter replied that they should be baptized. That day, there were three thousand people baptized and added to the church (Acts 2:41). This would serve as the foundation of the New Testament church in which growth aided by the Holy Spirit almost immediately started. This growth was started by a small group of disciples but was explosive, and it "added to the church daily" (Acts 2:47). This initial act served as the springboard that would propel the New Testament Church forward to evangelize and create disciples in other parts of the known world, so all might know the good news of Jesus Christ.

The Acts of the Apostles in the New Testament serves as a dramatic and fascinating description of the history of the first Christian church after the resurrection of Jesus Christ to the Christian Church. The book of Acts of the Apostles describes what the Great Commission referenced, God's new work on earth did not end with the resurrection of Jesus Christ. The work continues through the Holy Spirit that pours out on faithful followers. The disciples would grow from a small, frightened group to become a dynamic movement with Spirit-given power to turn "the world upside down" (Acts 17:6). The disciples' work after Pentecost described in Acts and the epistles record additional information about church growth, evangelism, and small groups. These things are profoundly useful for church growth.

In today's church, the mission has not changed. The church is still attempting to go into the world and make disciples by declaring the good news of Jesus Christ under the power and urging of the Holy Spirit to bring in new believers. Over the years, many churches across the country believe in evangelizing their community, so non-believers are aware of the Second Coming of Jesus Christ and their need to avail themselves of their only hope, Jesus Christ. This led churches to grow numerically and personally to participate in the mission to save souls. Today, growing the church numerically is still essential as it is still an outward indicator of the follow-through of the stated mission. However, most Christian churches today are either plateauing or declining. Is God stopping the church from growing because He seeks to discipline Her for not being faithful? No. The church remains stagnant because we have failed to implement biblical principles in evangelism. These principles would seem to include small groups, as even most individuals often would cite key verses including Acts 2:41-47 to establish the foundation for small group ministries.

While some church leaders acknowledge the importance of evangelism through small groups and biblical principles associated with it, they have yet to implement them into their churches actively. Many successful pastors have enjoyed sustained numerical growth in their ministries. Upon careful examination, they almost have used small groups exclusively at the center of their ministry often designing discipleship, worship, fellowship and other key launchpads from the concept. They believe that the small group's purpose is the same purpose of the church, which is spelled out in John 17:3. Specifically, the purpose of a small group's existence is to enable others to know God, and to allow God to be known. The formula for many successful ministries' evangelistic success is heavily dependent on small groups.

My belief is that small groups are not only biblical, but they are essential in the modern church. By looking at the book of Acts, you can see the extraordinary growth of the church and how they cared for and discipled them. It all started with small groups. Acts 2 is a clear description of small group evangelism in which new believers were able to "break bread in their homes and ate together with gladness of hearts" (Acts 2:46). The strategy of small groups led to exponential growth then, and it also can lead to exponential growth in your ministry.

The Christian church at large is genuinely in need of a solution for the continual demise of its stagnant evangelistic program and its inability to keep existing members in the pews. The church struggles to evangelize new believers and mobilize or keep its existing members. While the erosion of any church is generally a slow process that could take years, the inability to keep existing members, mobilize them in the community, and add new members means the church is in danger of becoming deceased. Small groups can provide the catalyst that propels substantial growth of the church, expands the Great Commission, and leads others to a relationship with Jesus Christ.

CHAPTER 1

WELCOME TO SMALL GROUP EVANGELISM!

Go into all the world and preach the gospel to all creation.
Mark 16:15 NASB

"Go means Go! All means all!"

Whether you are on a mission to increase fellowship, populate your church or grow spiritually by carrying out the mission of the church, this planner will help you stay focused on creating and starting a consistent small group.

What is evangelism?

If you ask five church members what evangelism is, you most likely will get five different answers. To some, evangelism means setting up a tent and holding a meeting where they talk about Jesus. To others, it might be helping the poor and disenfranchised. To others, evangelism means passing out literature about the Bible. Many people will have an idea of things that might be associated with evangelism, but they may not necessarily understand what evangelism *is.*. For our purposes, evangelism will be defined as "the sharing of the gospel by proclamation, acts of service, or any other means that gives people a chance to come into a personal relationship with Jesus Christ."

The gospel writers all rooted their story in evangelism or the message of Jesus Christ who came to Earth to deliver, teach, die, and rise again for all of us! Jesus wants everyone to spread the word. Jesus came so that we may live and have life more abundantly. Jesus wants people to know they can be part of God's Holy Kingdom and partake of everlasting life. He directs all His loyal followers to evangelize throughout Scripture. The great commission in Matthew 28:19-20, says, "Therefore go and make disciples of all nations, baptizing them in the name of the Father and of the Son and of the Holy Spirit, and teaching them to obey everything I have commanded you. And surely I am with you always, to the very end of the age." We are to spread this good news everywhere — to the ends of the Earth. The sharing of the good news of Jesus Christ by proclamation, acts of service, or any means that gives individuals a chance to come into a personal relationship with Jesus Christ is evangelism! The hope of performing evangelism is to draw oneself and others to become more and more like Jesus Christ or enrich your relationship and closeness with Jesus Christ.

Within the context of evangelism, a small group is a subset of people, usually from within an existing church, who band together with the main thrust of sharing the gospel by proclamation, acts of service or other means. In most churches there are usually small groups created by default like choirs, usher boards, women's ministries, youth departments, marriage ministries, singles ministries, etc. One could utilize these existing small groups or create a new small group depending on their vision. This planner assumes you are starting from scratch.

What's inside The Small Group Evangelism Planner

There are many elements involved in the planning, creation and successfully execution of an evangelistic small group. I have designed this planner with those elements in mind. I created structures to help break down your information and ideas in their related fields, while still allowing for your personal customization based on the context of your ministry. Think of it as freestyling within a framework and use this planner as you wish. The planner consists of the following components and templates:

- Small Group Compass
- Small Group Calendar Planning
- Small Group Checklist
- Small Group Brainstorming
- Small Group Planning Diary
- Notes Sections

There will be some suggestions made along the way as well as assumptions that may or may not hold true. Your goal should be to write down as much information as you can to plan and execute your small group using the planner as a resource.

Let's Stay Connected

Your purchase of The Small Group Planner comes with some resources to keep you connected with the author and others that are creating small groups. Not only can you connect via social media but by sending an email to John@realmomentsmedia.com you can be added to a monthly newsletter and private Facebook Group where you cna

CHAPTER 2

PLANNING TOOLS FOR SMALL GROUP EVANGELISM

For where two or three are Gathered in
my name, there I am among them.

Matthew 18:20 NASB

"God is in the midst."

Small Group Compass

C reating a Small group Compass will have more than just the basic information about your small group. It will help you focus on the original goals and interest you intended for your podcast.

When issues arise in your group, this compass will guide you from a core set of actions based upon your original vision.

Before filling in the below table completely, feel free to refer back to the chapter on planning and utilize the notes section of this book to brainstorm through some of the more thought-provoking questions. Once you feel you have the correct answers, write them in the designated field below. The more specific the better.

The basics of my Evangelistic Small Group

Group Name	Answer
Tag line	
Description	
Leader / Hosts	
Secondary Leaders / Hosts	
Place(s) to meet	
Schedule of meeting	
Time to meet	

Structure	
limitations	
Content and resources	
Interactions	
Initial members	
3 month goal	
6 month Goal	

Strategy for replication	
Deficiences	
Communication	
Other	
Other	
Other	
Other	

Small Group Checklist

Launching a small group consists of important tasks that cannot be missed. Below is a list of common tasks for when you're ready to launch your small group. Every small group is unique, therefore not all tasks items listed below are required, but optional. We have left space for you to add your own.

✧ Group Goal

✧ Name

✧ Purpose

✧ Binding Theme

✧ Mission Statement

✧ Funding

✧ Recruitment

✧ Schedule

✧ Structure / Communication

✧ Resources

✧ Interaction

✧ Potential members list

✧ Other

✧ Other

✧ Other

✧ Other

✧ Other

CHAPTER 3

SMALL GROUP EVANGELISM PLANNING CONSIDERATIONS

And they devoted themselves to the apostles' teaching and the fellowship, to the breaking of bread and the prayers. And awe[d] came upon every soul, and many wonders and signs were being done through the apostles. And all who believed were together and had all things in common. And they were selling their possessions and belongings and distributing the proceeds to all, as any had need. And day by day, attending the temple together and breaking bread in their homes, they received their food with glad and generous hearts, praising God and having favor with all the people. And the Lord added to their number day by day those who were being saved.

Where two or three are Gathered in my name, There I am among them

Acts 2:42-47 ESV

"Let the teaching and fellowship begin."

This chapter will go through all of the suggested areas defined in your planning tools sections. On the journey to planning your small group, you should utilize this area to think through specifics of your small group and even quickly jot down rational behind your decisions. Then transfer each final response to the actual planning tool. When all questions have been answered you are ready to launch your small group. Next to some of the areas we will provide a fictitious example of a small group to assist you in playing.

Group Goal: You have to decide what the goal of the group is going to be. Evangelistic Small Groups can have different group goals. A few examples include Disciple-making groups: for believers wanting to develop spiritual disciplines and go deep, Community Groups: for believers and non-believers, persons who want to build in-depth relationships with others, service Groups: for believers and non-believers who are serving alongside one another in ministry, Seeker Groups: groups led by a couple of believers but for non-believers. Groups that spend much time dealing with the issues non-believers are considering before coming to Christ, and Support Groups: groups for believers and non-believers that support attendees through personal difficulties. Group Goal: _____

_____

_____

_____

_____

_____

_____

Purpose Statement: You should immediately craft a purpose statement that will be a compelling purpose statement that can be used to drive the ministry and develop the core of your evangelistic small group. It should be short enough to be easily memorized and recalled. Purpose Statement: _____

_____

_____

_____

_____

_____

Name: While it might seem like a trivial item, the name of an evangelistic small group is important. The name doesn't have to be long or have some deep meaning but it should somehow be descriptive of your group and allow others to quickly identify you and or your mission. Examples of group names would be "Women's Small Group", "Kids for Christ", "Single Souls". Notice, that just by mentioning the name an individual can guess who is involved in the group and quite possibly the charge. Your group name:_____

_____

_____

_____

_____

_____

_____

Description: The description of your group can be a longer version of your purpose statement with additional detail you may have left out. Maybe it includes principles from scriptures, etc. Description: _____

_____

_____

_____

_____

_____

_____

_____

_____

_____

Mission statement: What is your overall mission? Lead others to christ? Develop fellowship? Heal the wounds of marriage relationships? This should be very short and concise statement that defines what you want to effect and or change moving forward. Mission statement: _____

_____

_____

_____

_____

_____

_____

_____

_____

_____

_____

_____

_____

Tag Line: A tag line is not necessary belt helpful If you plan to use for organizing or advertising the group. An example tagline would for women's small group ministry might be: "Assisting women in reaching their full potential today and tomorrow. Tag Line: _____

_____

_____

_____

_____

_____

_____

_____

_____

Leader / Hosts & Secondary Leader / Hosts: In most cases you are looking to start a group and will be its leader. However, in some cases you will be planning the group for someone else to lead. You need to identify the leader, host as will as secondary leaders or hosts. Keep in mind you will want spiritual leaders that will give and receive scriptural correction (Proverbs 19:20), serve others rather than only being served (Philippians 2:3-11), Follow the spiritual leadership of others (Hebrews 13:17), initiate forgiveness and reconciliation with others (Matthew 5:21-26) and Keep their word (Matthew 5:33-37). Leaders/ Hosts & secondary leader / host: _____

_____

_____

_____

_____

_____

_____

_____

Meeting Location(s): Where will the group meet? Keep in mind the group may meet in multiple locations. For example, maybe it moves from home to home or meets twice, once at a location for fellowship but a different location for ministry. Keep this in mind and don't be afraid to come back or write down TBD for To Be Determined if need be. Meeting Location(s): _____

_____

_____

_____

Meeting Times: What are times the group will meet. Again this may also be determined by the location and could be TBD. Meeting Times:_____

Suggested interactions: How will your group interact with each other and the community? Do you intend to interact directly with the community or is this a closed group? Suggested Interactions:

_____

_____

_____

_____

_____

_____

_____

_____

_____

_____

_____

_____

_____

_____

_____

_____

Structure: How will the group be structured? Will you have officers in place? Who will be responsible for what areas? All of these things should be thoroughly thought through. Structure: ____

_____

_____

_____

_____

_____

_____

_____

_____

_____

_____

Communication: Identify how you will communicate with the group. This means picking the best gorm of communication for all that will be involved. This may be utilizing a group email address, group text chat, message delivery service like call multiplier, or a third-party application like GroupMe. When you're figuring this out, be sure not to use a method that members will not have access to or this may create additional hardships. Group communication method: _____

_____

_____

_____

_____

_____

_____

_____

_____

Funding: How will the group get funding? Will it collect dues or be funded as an axillary of the church? Funding: _____

_____

_____

_____

_____

_____

_____

_____

_____

_____

_____

Limitations: What limits are there going to be on the group. What areas are you going to exclude or not focus on: _____

_____

_____

_____

_____

_____

_____

_____

_____

_____

_____

_____

_____

_____

_____

_____

_____

_____

Possible initial members: To start your group you will need assistance from others. You don't have to start with 50 members. Just a few will do. These first initial group members will be your core group and should firmly behind you as you press forward. Also keep in mind that you want to have backup or at least one secondary leader in your core group that can assist with the group as well as be available should the group grow large enough and need to be split up. Generally, you should come up with 3-12 people to start your group off, then gain agreement by communicating your idea about the group. Initial Members: _____

_____

_____

_____

_____

_____

_____

_____

_____

_____

_____

_____

_____

_____

_____

_____

_____

_____

_____

_____

_____

_____

Recruiting: How will you recruit core members and new members as you grow. This could be word of mouth, flyers, advertising or any number of ways. Recruiting: _____

_____

_____

_____

_____

_____

_____

_____

_____

_____

_____

_____

Group Schedule: As you start your group the meetings should be consistent and well scheduled. The time of the meeting should be consistent so participants can identify if they can attend and if its possible to schedule around other activities like jobs, families, etc. There is no way to accommodate or anticipate everyone's schedule so don't worry if some cannot attend. Maybe that is an opportunity for a new group to start up. An example meeting schedule would be the First and third Sunday of the month or the second and fourth Thursday of every month. Group Schedule _____

_____

_____

_____

_____

_____

_____

_____

Meeting expectations: The group members should know what is expected during the meeting. For example, a common format should be used at every meeting. While prayer should be utilized, due to the type of group and the location your meeting at, a fellowship meal or Bible study may not be possible. By setting expectation members know what to expect and how to successfully participate. This will assist in preventing the group from not being effective. Meeting expectations: _____

_____

_____

_____

_____

_____

_____

_____

Goals: 3 month & 6 month: What are your Goals that you intend to achieve over the next 3, 6, 9 or 12 months. _____

_____

_____

_____

_____

_____

_____

_____

_____

_____

_____

_____

_____

_____

_____

Strategy for replication: As your group grows how will your group replicate. For example, If your small group hits a certain number will you then spawn another small group that will be led by one of your assistance. Replication Strategy: _____

_____

_____

_____

_____

_____

_____

How to handle new members: As new members come into the group how will you great them and orientate them into the group? Will you have group helpers or people there to make them feel comfortable and a part of the group? New member assistance: _____

_____

_____

_____

_____

_____

_____

_____

_____

_____

_____

_____

_____

_____

_____

_____

Deficiencies: What areas are you or the group going to be deficient in? While this may seem counterintuitive, identifying group flaws or issues before they become a problem and stagnate the group will assist you later down the line: Deficiencies: _____

_____

_____

_____

_____

_____

_____

_____

_____

_____

_____

Other: There are some things that have been purposely left out of this list. It might depend on the type of group or your specific location. Use this space to identify those key or missing items or issue you want to address. _____

_____

_____

_____

_____

_____

_____

_____

_____

_____

_____

_____

_____

Small Group Notes

Small Group Notes

Small Group Notes

Small Group Notes

Small Group Notes

Small Group Notes

Small Group Notes

Small Group Notes

Small Group Notes

Small Group Notes

Small Group Notes

Small Group Notes

Small Group Notes

Small Group Notes

Small Group Notes

Small Group Notes

Small Group Resource Planning

Write a detailed description of the resources you plan to use.

_____

_____

_____

_____

_____

_____

_____

_____

_____

_____

_____

_____

_____

_____

_____

_____

_____

_____

Small Group Core Member Brainstorming

This area can be used with core members.
These are usually the secondary leaders / hosts.

Small Group Calendar

Month 1

SUN	MON	TUE	WED	THU	FRI	SAT

Month 2

SUN	MON	TUE	WED	THU	FRI	SAT

Month 3

SUN	MON	TUE	WED	THU	FRI	SAT

Month 4

SUN	MON	TUE	WED	THU	FRI	SAT

Month 5

SUN	MON	TUE	WED	THU	FRI	SAT

Month 6

SUN	MON	TUE	WED	THU	FRI	SAT

CHAPTER 4

KICK OFF MEETING FOR SMALL GROUP EVANGELISM

Take care, brothers, lest there be in any of you an evil, unbelieving heart, leading you to fall away from the living God. But exhort one another every day, as long as it is called "today," that none of you may be hardened by the deceitfulness of sin. For we have come to share in Christ, if indeed we hold our original confidence firm to the end.

Hebrews 3:12-14 ESV

"Exhort each other every day!"

ONE WEEK OR A FEW DAYS BEFORE THE FIRST MEETING

1. Make sure you have contacted all group members and that they know when, where and at what time the group is, as well as a little of what they can expect from the group.
2. Prepare the content of your lesson and go through it yourself.
3. Prepare to lead or guide the lesson. It is one thing to study the lesson yourself; it is another thing to lead it.
4. Pray for those coming. Ask God for wisdom about how He wants to work in their lives.

TWO DAYS BEFORE YOUR SMALL GROUP

1. Contact group members to remind them of the time and place. Be sure to let them know you are glad they are coming. Make sure they have your phone number.
2. Plan a good icebreaker to help group members start building relationships. An icebreaker is something that gets each group member talking and sharing early on. Choose one that works for any number of people. Check out some ideas for icebreakers.
3. Plan the specifics for your meeting. You have a limited amount of time to build relationships, cover content and pray. What portion of the time do you want to spend on

each aspect? Different levels of spiritual maturity among members will dictate different amounts of time for each part, and the balance of time will likely be different as the group grows and its members get to know one another.

4.   Pick up some refreshments. The first few weeks can be awkward as people get to know one another. There is nothing like a good snack to get people comfortable, loosened up and talking. Make it easy on yourself and buy something prepared.

THIRTY MINUTES BEFORE YOUR SMALL GROUP

1.   Be there early to review the lesson.

2.   Pray for your time and your group members, and ask the Lord to give you the ability to lead well.

3.   Turn your phone to vibrate to reduce the distractions (but keep it on in case someone gets lost and tries to call you).

4.   Make sure there are plenty of comfortable seats.

5.   Set out snacks.

6.   Send out last minute reminder texts to people.

CONDUCTING YOUR FIRST MEETING

Begin by introducing people to one another. Don't delay. Start with your icebreaker and then transition into your study. Be sure to end promptly.

In the first meeting, focus on building relationships. That's not to say you should minimize the Bible, but if the people in the group don't know each other, it's important that they learn more about each other. Read "How to Build Community in Your Small Group" for ideas on how to continue to build community over time.

Read "Your First Group Meeting" for more tips.

AFTER THE FIRST MEETING

1. Call the group members and ask them how things are going. Ask them specifics about the things they shared in the group.

2. Serve them. If someone in the group expressed a need, try to meet it — a ride to a job interview, a meal on a hectic day, a call to follow up a prayer request, etc.

3. Do something fun. Meet people for lunch, sit with them at church, or greet them with a cup of coffee.

4. Evaluate how it went and make any necessary changes before the next week.

EVALUATE YOUR MEETING

1. How did you see God at work during the meeting? Take time to thank Him for all He did.

2. Did everyone show up?
   o Did people who had expressed interest but didn't show up contact you before or after the meeting to tell you why?
   o Is there anything you can do to help more people come in the future?
   o If people forgot, you could call them an hour before.
   o If the time/place isn't convenient for multiple people who are interested, could you change it?

3. Were you prepared? Did you feel confident and at ease?

4. Did you have an attitude of expectancy? Were you prepared for everyone who came?

5. Did you create a warm atmosphere? Did people seem comfortable? (Some people may feel awkward regardless of how welcoming you are, but if most people seemed relaxed and open, that's a good indication you created a good environment).

6. What other adjustments do you need to make?

PLAN THE NEXT FEW MEETINGS

Icebreakers

Choose an icebreaker for each meeting. Choose icebreakers that will work for both small and large groups. Choose activities that will help people get to know each other but won't feel intrusive for people who may not feel comfortable opening up right away.

Content

You want your content to have continuity, but you also want each lesson to be able to stand alone if someone misses a meeting or someone new comes. Don't discourage your group members by making them feel lost if they didn't make a previous meeting.

At the same time, having a theme or a topic for several weeks in a row can help the group feel more consistent. One idea is to stick to the fundamentals of the Christian faith, which will be accessible to everyone.

If you are working with predetermined content, such as questions based on weekly sermons or a book, make sure that anyone who comes can still participate in the discussion. If someone didn't hear the sermon or didn't read the chapter, give a summary at the beginning or write up a summary and give everyone a few minutes to read it before the discussion. Be sure to explain anything that may not be clear during the discussion, such as quotations or references.

Small groups can be a great opportunity for members to invite friends, but group members may not feel comfortable inviting people if guests will have to listen to a sermon or read a chapter from a book to participate.

CHAPTER 5

EXAMPLE PLAN
FOR SMALL GROUP
EVANGELISM

Beloved, if God so loved us, we also ought to love
one another. No one has ever seen God; if we
love one another, God abides in us and his love
is perfected in us. By this we know that we abide
in him and he in us, because he has given us of
his Spirit.

1 John 4:11-13 ESV

"Love, then love some more!"

The below plan is simply an example plan that could be used to jumpstart your small group. While this plan is meant to be enacted as part of the local congregation, it does not have to be limited to that scope. It simply could be started as a side project by any Christian group that is operating from a home.

PARTICIPANTS

Participants should be selected based upon the group's needs. Groups should consider inviting couples, men, and people from a desired age group. Additionally, they should have a desired number of members in mind. In the example, our participants will be members of the same church with a maximum starting number of twelve members. The ages of the participants are of no consequence; however, because transportation may be an issue, and the group seeks to add younger adults , the specified participants will be between the ages of eighteen to fifty. While more than the twelve core members may start attending the functions and grow the small group, the starting group is limited to the twelve individuals. Start recruiting your participants. Make them aware of the goal or mission of the small group and ask them to commit themselves to the initial first run which will be a thirteen-week process. Call each participant and confirm the initial meeting time, place, and location.

GATHERING AND EVENTS

The small group example has a commitment to both personal community gatherings and weekly evangelistic events over a thirteen-week period. There will be two weekly meetings. The first meeting will be a core group gathering to build community and discuss evangelism. These meetings will take place on Saturday afternoons and will be scheduled in either the church fellowship hall or a participant's home. At the community meeting, participants will share a full meal including an entrée, refreshments, and snacks.

Multiple options will be made available for those who have specific dietary concerns. After eating, the core curriculum will be taught to emphasize evangelism in the attendees' lives. After the first meeting, new individuals will be able to join the core team meeting. This meeting will take approximately two hours for the meal and the presentation of the curriculum.

The second meeting will be a community outreach event. The outreach events are designed to take the small group out into the community to evangelize and assist in particular community-based efforts. The end goal is to allow people to work towards the good of others and share their faith while working as part of a small group. The outreach events will occur on Thursdays or Sundays, and usually, they will last for two to three hours. These events can be planned and executed by the small group leader or by a third party with whom the group is working. For example, this work can include working in a soup kitchen that is already established or performing a Toys for Tots drive. Even if they are a part of a greater effort, the group will attempt to stay together as much as possible.

Within the thirteen weeks, there will be a total of twenty-six meetings and a conclusion worship service that occurs at the church. The total order and goals of the twenty-six meetings are to talk about a specific topic, which in our example, is personal evangelism and perform one act of community service per week. Below is an outline you can adapt to your group:

Week 1: The goal for week one is to discuss the goals of the training group, its schedule, and the obligations for each meeting. The group's aim is to learn the ideas and skills to do small group evangelism, to develop a warm, caring group to encourage outreach, and to participate in all weekly group events.

Small Group Gathering: Saturday at fellowship hall directly after service.

      i.   Meal (45 Minutes)

      ii.   Introduction (5 Minutes)

      iii. Getting to Know One Another (30 minutes): Provide name and answer and ice breaker question that will be provided.

      iv. Principles of Evangelism (40 minutes): Talk about the topics below:

          1.   Great Commission

          2.   Every member is a minister

          3.   God's role in evangelism

          4.   Hopes and fears of evangelism

   a.   Outreach Event: Thursday 6PM-8PM

      v.   Food Pantry Food Distribution

Week 2: Continue to develop group dynamics as well as have each member identify his or her spiritual gifts and share how those gifts can be effective in evangelism.

Small Group Gathering: Saturday at fellowship hall directly after service

      i.   Meal (45 Minutes)

      ii.   Introduction (5 Minutes)

      iii. Spiritual Gifts

          1.   Introduction (5 minutes)

          2.   Principles of Spiritual gifts (20 minutes)

        3.   Spiritual Gifts and Evangelism (20 minutes)

        4.   Spiritual Gifts Survey and Scoring (60 minutes)

        5.   Concluding Remarks (15 minutes)

  b.   Outreach Event: Thursday 6PM-8PM

    iv.   Food Pantry Food Distribution

Week 3: This week will be focused on witnessing. Members need to understand the principles of inviting someone to Christ and developing their own personal testimony that they can share.

Small Group Gathering: Saturday at fellowship hall directly after service

    i.   Meal (45 Minutes)
    ii.   Introduction (5 Minutes)
    iii.   Witnessing

        1.   Introduction (5 minutes)

        2.   Principles of invitation (20 minutes)

        3.   What is my witness (20 minutes)

        4.   Developing your witness story and invitation (60 minutes)

        5.   Concluding Remarks (15 minutes)

  c.   Outreach Event: Thursday 6PM-8PM

    iv.   Food Pantry Food Distribution

Week 4: This week will be about learning how to share and listen to others and their life experiences, how to share personally what they are experiencing, and how to hear and encourage others by providing feedback without judgment.

Small Group Gathering: Saturday at fellowship hall directly after service

      i. Meal (45 Minutes)
      ii. Introduction (5 Minutes)
      iii. Christian conversation
            1. Introduction (5 minutes)
            2. Listening Exercise (20 minutes)
            3. Caring Exercise (20 minutes)
            4. Sharing Exercise (60 minutes)
            5. Concluding Remarks (15 minutes)

    d. Outreach Event: Thursday 6PM–8PM

      v. Food Pantry Food Distribution

Week 5: This week focuses on what prayer is, how to intercede on someone's behalf, and what group prayer is. At the end, the small group will choose and plan an activity to perform during Week 9 that is of interest to the group.

Small Group Gathering: Saturday at fellowship hall directly after service

      i. Meal (45 Minutes)
      ii. Introduction (5 Minutes)
      iii. Prayer and planning
            1. Introduction (5 minutes)

        2.   Principles of Prayer (20 minutes)

        3.   Group Prayer (20 minutes)

        4.   Planning Outreach Event(s) (60 minutes)

        5.   Concluding Remarks (15 minutes)

    e.   Outreach Event: Thursday 6PM-8PM

        iv.   Food Pantry Food Distribution

Week 6: During this week the small group will put prayer as a group into practice. Then, they will spend a small amount of time talking about the group and the way things are going thus far. Finally, they will plan an outreach activity to perform during week 10.

Small Group Gathering: Saturday at fellowship hall directly after service

      i.   Meal (45 Minutes)

      ii.   Introduction (5 Minutes)

      iii.   Prayer, Process and Plan

          1.   Introduction (5 minutes)

          2.   Group Prayer (20 minutes)

          3.   Discuss the Group (20 minutes)

          4.   Plan Outreach Events (60 minutes)

          5.   Concluding Remarks (15 minutes)

    f.   Outreach Event: Thursday 6PM-8PM

        iv.   Food Pantry Food Distribution

Week 7: During this week, the group will seek to get a better understanding of Jesus and the gospel. They will learn why His death and resurrection are good news and why those events are important? They will explore what He accomplished specifically and how it is both corporate and personal.

Small Group Gathering: Saturday at fellowship hall directly after service

      i.   Meal (45 Minutes)

      ii.   Introduction (5 Minutes)

      iii. Evaluation (10 minutes)

      iv. Who is Jesus to me?

           1.   Introduction (5 minutes)

           2.   Who is Jesus in the Bible? (10 minutes)

           3.   What did Jesus accomplish? (15 minutes)

           4.   Why is that important? (10 minutes)

           5.   Making Jesus Personal (15)

           6.   Concluding Remarks (5 minutes)

    g.   Outreach Event: Thursday 6PM-8PM

      v.   Food Pantry Food Distribution

Week 8: This week is about discussing how they can enter into a relationship with Jesus Christ and what has changed. The goal is to get people to see that while the members of the group have relationships with God, those relationships can mean different things.

Small Group Gathering: Saturday at fellowship hall directly after service

    i.   Meal (45 Minutes)
    ii.   Introduction (5 Minutes)
    iii. Personal Journey

        1.   Introduction (5 minutes)

        2.   How did you get to know Christ? (40 minutes)

        3.   What can you say about that to others? (20 minutes)

        4.   Concluding Remarks (5 minutes)

    h.   Outreach Event: Thursday 6PM-8PM

    iv.   Food Pantry Food Distribution

Week 9: This week is about praying and discussing the group. Two-thirds of the research project is now complete. What has been accomplished? How does everyone feel? What still needs to be done? Another planning session will take place to discuss an outreach event for Week 11 of the group's choosing.

Small Group Gathering: Saturday at fellowship hall directly after service

    i.   Meal (45 Minutes)
    ii.   Introduction (5 Minutes)
    iii. Prayer, Process and Plan II

        1.   Introduction (5 minutes)

        2.   Group Prayer (20 minutes)

        3.   Discuss the Group (20 minutes)

        4.   Plan Outreach Events (60 minutes)

        5.   Concluding Remarks (15 minutes)

     i.   Outreach Event: Thursday 6PM-8PM

       iv.   Provided by group from Week 5.

Week 10: The goal of this week is to shift to a book that is focused on Christ. The study and emphasis will be on Chapter 1 of the book, *Steps to Christ*, that expounds upon the idea of God's love for man. (He sent his only begotten Son, etc.)

Small Group Gathering: Saturday at fellowship hall directly after service

     i.   Meal (45 Minutes)
     ii.   Introduction (5 Minutes)
    iii.   *Steps to Christ* Book Chapter 1
         1.   Introduction (5 minutes)
         2.   Group Prayer (10 minutes)
         3.   Discuss the Book (45 minutes)
         4.   Concluding Remarks (10 minutes)

    j.   Outreach Event: Thursday 6PM-8PM

       iv.   Provided by the group from Week 6.

Week 11: The goal of this week is to continue the group study on the book, *Steps to Christ*. Chapter 2 expounds on the concept of sinners who are in need of Christ.

Small Group Gathering: Saturday at fellowship hall directly after service

     i.   Meal (45 Minutes)
     ii.   Introduction (5 Minutes)
    iii.   *Steps to Christ* Chapter 2
         1.   Introduction (5 minutes)

2. Group Prayer (10 minutes)
3. Discuss the Book (45 minutes)
4. Concluding Remarks (10 minutes)

k. Outreach Event: Thursday 6PM-8PM

iv. Provided by the group from Week 9.

Week 12: The goal of this week is to continue the group study on the book, *Steps to Christ*. Chapter 3 discusses repentance.

Small Group Gathering: Saturday at fellowship hall directly after service

i. Meal (45 Minutes)
ii. Introduction (5 Minutes)
iii. *Steps to Christ* Chapter 3
    1. Introduction (5 minutes)
    2. Group Prayer (10 minutes)
    3. Discuss the Book (45 minutes)
    4. Concluding Remarks (10 minutes)

l. Outreach Event: Thursday 6PM-8PM

iv. Food Pantry Food Distribution

Week 13: The goal of this week is to finalize the group's activities, take surveys, and give comments, suggestions, etc. Invite everyone to the following week's worship service to celebrate and plan for future small group sessions.

Small Group Gathering: Saturday at fellowship hall directly after service

      i.   Meal (45 Minutes)
      ii.   Introduction (5 Minutes)
      iii. What's Next?
           1.   Introduction (5 minutes)
           2.   Group Prayer (10 minutes)
           3.   Discuss the Group and Surveys (10 minutes)
           4.   Plan What's Next (60 minutes)
           5.   Concluding Remarks (5 minutes)

   m. Outreach Event: Thursday 6PM-8PM
      iv. Food Pantry Food Distribution

   n. Sabbath Worship
      v.   Congratulate and replicate results

At the culmination or conclusion to the thirteen-week session will be a "Friends and Family" service held at the church. During this service's worship program, individuals will be recognized for their achievement and participation in the thirteen-week session. All individuals involved will be recognized including the core team, people who joined the effort, and those who may have participated in response to the efforts of the team.

CHAPTER 6

NOTES

Do your best to present yourself to God as one approved, a worker who has no need to be ashamed, rightly handling the word of truth.

1 John 4:11-13 ESV

"Keep the Faith!"

About the Author

Dr. John R. Sconiers, II, DMin, is a senior pastor, preacher, mentor, and evangelism coordinator. His education includes DMin in evangelism and church planting, DIT in Security, MAPM (MDIV Equivalent), MIS Security, BSIT as well as postgraduate work in counseling. He also holds numerous certifications and has hosted training sessions. Dr. Sconiers has lived and preached in various parts of the world and has a passion for seeing lives transformed by the power of the Holy Spirit and seeks to point others to the good news of Jesus Christ. Dr. Sconiers currently serves as a senior pastor in the North Georgia area. He is married to one wife, Nicole, and they share five amazing children.

Connect with Dr. Sconiers

You can connect with Dr. John R Sconiers II via:

Instagram: @johnsconiers

Twitter: @johnsconiers

YouTube: @JohnSconiers

Email: John@realmomentsmedia.com

Website: http://www.johnsconiers2.com

www.ingramcontent.com/pod-product-compliance
Lightning Source LLC
Chambersburg PA
CBHW070454130626
46553CB00006B/2416